# A THOUSAND VESSELS

# A THOUSAND VESSELS

POEMS

*Tania Runyan*

WORDFARM

SEATTLE, WASHINGTON

WordFarm
2816 E. Spring St.
Seattle, WA 98122
www.wordfarm.net
info@wordfarm.net

Cover Image: iStockphoto
Cover Design: Andrew Craft

USA ISBN-13: 978-1-60226-009-2
USA ISBN-10: 1-60226-009-5
Printed in the United States of America
First Edition: 2011

---

Library of Congress Cataloging-in-Publication Data

Runyan, Tania.
 A thousand vessels : poems / Tania Runyan.
   p. cm.
 ISBN-13: 978-1-60226-009-2 (pbk.)
 ISBN-10: 1-60226-009-5 (pbk.)
 I. Title.
 PS3618.U5668T46 2011
 811'.6--dc23
                                                                    2011035220

---

P  10  9  8  7  6  5  4  3  2  1
Y  16  15  14  13  12  11

# Acknowledgments

*Bottomfish:* Honeymooning in Monterey Bay

*The Christian Century:* The Empty Tomb

*Christianity and Literature:* Queen Esther's Name Change

*The Comstock Review:* The Birth of Cain

*Confrontation:* The Possession of Mary Magdalene

*Innisfree:* Sarah Considers the Stars

*Literature and Belief:* I Find the Messiah, Thirst

*The Mennonite:* After the Annunciation, Jairus' Daughter

*Nimrod:* Drift (as The Hiding Place)

*Poetry:* The Bee Box

*Prism Review:* July Afternoon

*Silk Road:* Beach Walk

*Willow Review:* Strange Land, Bamboo, Keeping My Daughter, Easter, Life Outside, Mary Magdalene, Boaz Watches Ruth in the Fields, Ruth Speaks to Naomi

*Willow Springs:* Mary at the Nativity, The Wedding at Cana

# Contents

EVE

# Genesis

May splays its colors over the burbs.
I cannot stop staring
at the six hundred magenta tulips
bordering Century Corporate Park.
Sunlight spills across slick granite signs,
and torpid Canada Geese
who gave up on migration years ago
gather to graze on rolled-out carpets.

Yes, I have been fooled.
My heart believes something wild
will come of this freshly dug pond.
But what if this place became itself again—
tangle of switch grass, cattails, and blazing star
hissing and bellowing without edge?
Could I survive the terror of waking first?
Could I touch, cut a path, and name?

# Life Outside

To punish me, Adam has taken over
the trees: *Don't touch* any *this time*.
He lets the ripe fruit fall and dissolve
in the grass. I envy those flies
that just ride their wings into sweetness.

What do I say? I wish I could return to the tree
and turn away. I wish we could lie
naked in a field and nibble figs.
Now my stomach stirs like rocks
in a river. I can only wait
for him to pull a few roots and toss them
over his shoulder: *Eat.*

He is becoming the earth again.
It sifts through his hair
and settles in the creases of his skin.
His back ripples under the sun
like the mountains baking in the distance.

Sometimes, he stops and looks up,
as if a voice were breaking
through the trees. For a moment I see
his eyes, then they float over my shoulder,
as if another woman stood behind me,
beckoning him toward paradise.

# The Birth of Cain

Pain, He warned. But how
could I imagine it?

I thought when the time came
I would steal into the myrrh
like a mother gazelle, my belly
a low moon in the branches.
A soft birth, rustle of leaves.
Suckling, sleep, stars.

But one morning I broke
like a thundercloud in a field.
A lion tore through my body,
and the lion caught fire.
Everything I was—forests,
mountains, Adam—everything
I had ever thought or spoken
melted in the rhythmic flames.

How could I move again
to gather fruit and stones?
How could I become the mother
of the living, when the Lord
was unmaking me, burning me
back down to a bone?

# My Daughter's Hands

When did you hatch these pink birds
that alight on everything in the house?
They land on power cords and houseplants,
perch between the window blinds.

At communion, I hold you on my lap
as I take a cup from the silver tray.
Every muscle in your body strains.
You want nothing more in this world,
love nothing as you love this purple vial.
Color swims there. Light bounces.
You whimper, stretch and shriek.

People turn. Yet I know the moment I say *no*
your world will begin to go wrong.
You will learn that most bright things
are never meant to be touched
and have purposes other than your joy.
You will learn the tension in my neck
as I shake my head to the beautiful movements
of your flesh. You will swim against
the current of my voice jutted with stone eyes.
And eventually, even when we embrace,
a curtain will fall between us
like the thinnest, coldest silk.

So, child, take the cup and let it splash;
suck the sweet plastic and grin.
May your saliva roll down your chin
and neck, flicker on your fingers
that have just this brief time
to fly around the world.

# Bamboo

Four months ago
my husband carried this plastic cup
to the pick-up zone,
promising a corner forest
in our living room.
He had bought the cuttings
at a California street fair,
holding the cup steady
through a drive and two flights,
careful not to damage
the unrolling Y's of new leaves.
The stems haven't grown,
but he assures me
they will sprout exuberantly
if we keep the cup lit,
douse the roots with water
and remember the reward
of towering branches and lush blades,
the rustling of imagined cranes.
But I enjoy holding the bamboo
fixed in this moment,
when my husband shuffled
off the plane in celebration
of another span together,
the green question of our lives
alight and unfolding before us.

SARAH

# The Dangerous Wife

*"I know what a beautiful woman you are. When the Egyptians see you, they will say, 'This is his wife.' Then they will kill me but will let you live."*

−Genesis 12: 11-12, Abram to Sarai

What part of her beauty made him fear for his life
the most? The heaps of black hair draping her arms
as she bent into the vines for grapes? Ankles darting
like slender fish under the hem of an indigo tunic?

The men couldn't help it, of course. When Sarai stood
staring into the Nile, Pharaoh wanted to slide his fingers
along the mountains and canyons of her face, down
into the lush shadows. So Abram called her *sister* and let her
enter the palace as servants paid him cattle and sheep.

At sunset, he wandered alone through the market. Plain women
seemed to be everywhere, laughing, slapping the flanks
of his cattle. Lucky husbands, he thought. No need to fear
the women whose cracked feet spilled over the edges
of their sandals, whose lips disappeared in concentration
as they scrubbed their clothes in the river. They carried
the dust of the village in their hair. They balanced pots of water
on their fleshy hips and returned to their faithful homes.

# Sarah Considers the Stars

After Abraham fell asleep,
she pulled her cloak

around her shoulders
and walked out to stare

at the night. Stars collected
in the crevices of mountains.

They spilled into the oak groves
and clung to the branches.

And when she spread her hands
to the sky, they rested in the sags

of flesh between her fingers.
The world is dripping with stars,

she thought, and still not one
belongs to me. She considered

hating them. She considered
wishing a heavenly storm

to drown them. But she only
murmured *I am through*

and walked off, holding
a sudden sharpness in her side,

as if a star had dislodged
there and, turning and scraping

and shining its path, settled
into the bare sky of her body.

# The Return of Abraham and Isaac

Forgive, Lord, forgive.
Do not force Abraham back
to hold the blade above
his whimpering son, to kiss him
as the blood runs to his lips.
If you let him live,
I will lie on the ground
before you. My heart
will beat against the earth;
I will sweat into the grass
and bleed into the soil. I will
keep everything alive for you:
figs, myrtles, lizards, spiders—
even the small brown locust
you must have loved in the quiet
night as you formed its wings
      from nothing.

# Keeping My Daughter

Every morning we sit in a diagonal of sunlight.
She swings her legs in the high chair, pushing bananas

into her cheeks. I watch each movement
with vigilance. It can't go this well forever.

Soon I will be asked to give her up—
to the electric shocks of words synapsing

in her brain, to the accumulation of dark memories
filing in the grooves. I will have to give her

to the strangers who will bump her on the sidewalk
and move on—as if her body were not some miracle,

to the hundreds of cars and planes traveling
over distant, churning surfaces. I will give her

to the teacher rolling her eyes, to the HR head
shoving her résumé under an old coffee cup,

to the man who will touch her face the day after
touching another woman's face,

to the cells in her own body
that may spin out of orbit and consume her.

She slaps the tray with her fat palms.
I slice more bananas, top off the milk in her cup.

We must stay here as long as we can, balanced
on this precipice of light. The moment I let go,

the knife will come down—no ram in the thicket to save us.

DINAH

# The Rape of Dinah

*When Shechem . . . saw her, he took her and violated her.*
*His heart was drawn to Dinah daughter of Jacob, and*
*he spoke tenderly to her. And Shechem said to his father*
*Hamor, "Get me this girl as my wife."*
−Genesis 34: 2-4

Some time after ripping her tunic,
seizing her breasts with one hand
and entering her with the roughness
of a sandstorm, leaving her
to gape at the indifferent stars
as she staggered home to the valley,
he decided that he loved her.

I will bring her back, he resolved.
I will lay hyacinths on my bed
and let her dress fall softly
from her shoulders. Surely
she will smile then. Surely
she will forgive my body
when it clutches hers again.

# Dinah After the Revenge

*Dinah's brothers took their swords and attacked the
unsuspecting city, killing every male. . . . They looted the
city where their sister had been defiled.*
—Genesis 34: 25-27

I did not want people to die for me.
I wanted to go off alone

to watch the sparrows cluster in the trees.
Now to get a pot of water

I must trudge through a pasture of bodies.
Men lie beneath the heft of their cattle,

slump beside the boulders they thought
would hide them. They have no privacy

in death, their secrecy of blood
spreading in the sand. A few still live,

motionless but for their grinding teeth.
Men, I understand this. When you are torn,

everything sears your body—
wind, sunlight, the rumble of passing feet.

You become a sieve for the careless world,
catching its stones in your mesh.

# *Drift*

At last, April. We drive past the forest preserve,
treetops simmering green. I roll down the window
and press my palm to the wind.

I've read that in spring, young girls are driven
to places like these, forced to huddle under damp logs.
Some are thirteen, some are ten, some are six—
shivering in stilettos and halter tops.
They draw daisies in the dirt with sticks
as they wait for the men to appear at twilight.

The girls teach themselves to float away,
drifting to the canopy of branches.
One girl becomes a wisp of cloud;
one becomes a squirrel. One becomes a sparrow,
flitting among the open spaces
until she alights on a bud. She perches there
and refuses to move. When the wind tosses
the branch, she dips and sails with it, oblivious
to the whimpers below, the sudden pops
of raindrops, the rush of passing cars.

# Child Sex Offenders

We forget they live among us,
dragging their garbage to the curb,
sweeping snow from their windshields.

They scuffle through express lanes
with orange juice and magazines,
faces disappearing in the dark.

In their other world, they live
on the county website, photos posted
with their addresses and crimes.

Most stare straight ahead,
hair wild with grief.
Some raise their chins in defiance.

One looks upward with a small smile,
as if trying to remember something wonderful
that happened long ago. A luminous

Christmas morning when his father
embraced him, a teacher's scrawled *Bravo*
on a spelling test. A homemade sailboat

that caught the wind for a moment
and swept along the river, eternity
in front of it, the sun in its paper hull.

RUTH

# Ruth Speaks to Naomi

*"Where you go I will go, and where you stay I will stay.*
*Your people will be my people and your God my God."*
–Ruth 1:16

Really, there is not much to love
in this world. Maybe sparrows,
children laughing in the morning.

But—your God forgive me—
if I knew I had to sleep forever tonight,
my tired heart would survive it.

We are widows now, the shriveled leaves
that blow along the rooftops.
We are worth nothing

but the measure of loneliness
we can remove from each other.
Of course I must follow you,

Naomi, from Moab to Bethlehem,
to the musty corner of our home,
where we will boil the grain and sweep the dirt,

comb each other's hair in the evening
and feel the coarse curls fall
between our fingers.

# Strange Land

At nineteen, I convinced myself of imminent death.
I was ripe for tragedy, draped in the future
and beautiful long hair. So when I got lost on a hike
and stumbled to a creek of wild foxglove,
I thought, of course the rangers will find my body
in this paradise of leafy shadows,
bees turning in the flowers like amber stones.

I tried to pray, waiting for the bear to rumble
through the branches, the earthquake to dislodge boulders
on my neck. An hour passed. Insects ascended my sandals.
The foxglove blazed and pitched with no notice of me.
I might as well give up, I thought, and crawl
into these spotted throats to either drown in sweetness
or be flung out by the winds. Just keep walking
into whatever strange land God lays before me
to gather his blessings like petals and stones,
fallen dragonflies shimmering in the mud.

# Boaz Watches Ruth in the Fields

There is something holy in the way
she bends to the ground
and lifts each stalk like a child.

Her hair sweeps the soil,
trapping chaff in its curls.
How her fingers pierce the fields

like rays of light! I believe
she would glean here forever.
Even at sundown,

as the harvesters slump
beneath the sheaves on their backs,
she steps lightly to our meal

of roasted grain. She sighs deeply
with each bite, as if the barley
were part of her body,

finally reunited with its home
of sweet earth and sunlight,
ready to smolder and burst into the sky.

# Honeymooning in Monterey Bay

I imagined we'd never leave our room
at the Sandpiper Inn, our bodies separating
only for refills of Chardonnay and massage oil.

But we wandered Cannery Row, snapping pictures
of fat sea lions, smokestacks, my arm around
Steinbeck's shoulders. We entered the aquarium,
expecting long bodies gliding in circles
in massive tanks, water exploding
from blow holes, but found only fiberglass
dolphins and orcas hanging above us,
and tide pool after tide pool of sea anemones.
We didn't bother letting them suck our fingers.
A tank of sardines glimmered like a foil sheet,
ten thousand pivoting in the same direction.
Where was the great white, barracuda,
tentacles of a giant squid curling on the glass?
Deflated puffer fish lurked in a kelp forest.
Even the otters slept, dozens of untouched oysters
sinking to the floor.

I said we should go, remembering my lingerie,
but you strayed to a long counter of microscopes
and motioned me over, your arm brushing my breast
as you pointed to the sign: "Radiolarian Protozoa."
We took turns behind the lens, the skeletons
forming a latticework of cones and spheres,
silica arrows weaving through the openings,
holding the bodies together for good.

# The Threshing Floor

*"Wash and perfume yourself, and put on your best clothes.
Then go down to the threshing floor, but don't let him know
you are there. . . . Go and uncover his feet and lie down.
He will tell you what to do."*
—Ruth 3:2-4, Naomi to Ruth

She stirs in the heat of the harvest dawn,
lost in a dream of blue linen and myrrh.
Chaff sticks to her hair like moth wings.
Goat hooves shuffle the hay.

His feet poke out from the blanket,
heels cracked open like the Moab desert,
thickets of white hair curling on his toes.
She has just stopped missing her husband's feet,

the lean, brown knuckles that pressed against her
for seven years. She has begun to wake
each morning and stretch her limbs
like a great cedar tree, the warm sorrows

of widowhood surging through her body.
Now Boaz will take her in marriage,
and their feet will be one. For many thousand nights
her toes will wedge inside his knee

as she shifts and turns for comfort.
His calluses will whisper on her skin
from stars to dawn. His nails will cut.
She will never be alone.

ESTHER

# Beach Walk

*"Let a search be made for beautiful young virgins for the king."*
–Esther 2:2-4

I wore my leopard bikini like the mannequin
at Bullock's: shoulders back, breasts out,
fingertips light on my hips. Dina swiveled
her buttocks in a fuchsia French-cut
that pointed like an arrow between her thighs.

We drifted along the shore, saying nothing
as the sand sucked our glittering toenails.
When we neared the lifeguard station, I took my cue
and giggled loudly; Dina tossed the heavy rope
of her braid and spread out our towels.
A dozen girls lay there, still as downed soldiers.
The lifeguard stared into the water.

A hundred yards out, the boys rode the clear
green waves. They yelped and spun their boards,
raking their hair from their tanned faces
as the ocean trembled on their bodies.

The guard never spoke to us, but we still
imagined ourselves smoldering in his mind.
Layers of sweat and oil thickened on our skin
like glaze. The sun sank closer, closer
to the water until we could no longer move.

# Queen Esther's Name Change

*—Hadassah (Myrtle) to Esther (Star)*

With one word they have hurled me
to the heavens. I cannot believe

in these creatures that flicker to their deaths
each morning like the palace lamps.

Better the myrtles I used to visit
as an orphan. I thought I too had rooted

in the ground. I tucked the glossy leaves
in the folds of my dress, let the sweet oil

ooze between my fingers.
Now the eunuchs swarm like locusts.

They line my eyes with kohl,
drizzle cold perfume on my neck.

Better the fragrant myrtle petals
I used to shake into my hair,

the fine soil dusting my skin
as I napped beneath the branches.

At night, I hear nothing but chatter
about the king. The concubines slink around

the chamber, admiring the shiny edges
of their bodies. I stare into the sky, where starlight

bursts like the stamens of myrtle flowers,
calling me to be lonely and beautiful again.

# Esther Before the Throne

*"For if you remain silent at this time, relief and deliverance*
*for the Jews will arise from another place. . . . And who*
*knows but that you have come to royal position for such a*
*time as this?"*
—Esther 4:14, Mordecai to Esther


*Approach,* Xerxes booms, and extends
the royal scepter. I can only stare
at the tiny hairs on my fingers
stretching toward the light like seedlings.
Do they know they belong to my body?
Do they care if I stand or walk?

On the palace roof, I believe, a bird
is weaving her nest. Somewhere, a new cedar
is pushing through the rocks
to begin its mysterious purpose in the world.

*Now,* he demands, but I cannot bring myself
to touch the golden point. A dying moth
scuttles around the foot of the throne.
Dust motes float in the sunlight.

How do I just throw myself
into history, Lord? How do I step forward
when everything else falls so easily
into place, faithful and unknowing
in its movements, for such a time as this?

# Esther's Banquet

For nights she lay breathless,
the eyes of frightened children
blinking on her walls.
She imagined the wails of mothers
as Haman's swords

came down on infant necks,
the gasps of dying men
dragging themselves to cover
their families with their bodies.
So when Haman clambered

to her couch to plead for mercy,
it should have been easy
for her to throw another chunk of calf
on her plate and watch him
get dragged to the gallows.

But as he clenched her feet
and wept, hair raging
into his face, she thought,
how exhilarating it would be
to say, *Fine, I will let you go,*

and watch his eyes widen with wonder.
Then the delirious crying
and laughter, tears running down
his neck and trembling hands,
the frenzy of wine and flowers.

Oh, to give that gift,
to speak a life back into being

(even if in a day
he would plot and kill again):
to have no other duty

but to bless whomever stands
in front of you, your hands
behind your head
as you lie down at night,
ignorant of the world's schemes.

# For Such a Time as This

Because my mother was still pushing
at midnight, the nurse stayed past her shift
and did not take the highway
when the drunk spun across three lanes.
The boy I caught cheating
from my spelling test in fifth grade
had a repentant epiphany
and grew up to feed orphans in Mali.
And years later, when my missed free throw
lost the game, the other team stayed up
to celebrate, preventing their point guard
from journaling her suicide plans.

If life is nothing more than being on Earth
in a certain place at a certain time,
I have lived it well: signing up for the class
that saved the adjunct's apartment.
Adopting the cat that would have been
smashed on a country road
had the next woman peered into the cage.
Creating my daughter who stirs in her crib
as the rain spatters her window,
her body exerting force on all the matter
in the universe, keeping it in place.

MARY

# El Train Magnificat

Just when I think I've entered my rest,
the dull glare of the office two blocks behind me,
a woman under the Wells Street tracks
opens her arms and shouts, *Lord, I thank you!*
Her massive breasts quake in a gray T-shirt;
a sprig of hair trembles in a rubber band.
*You made* me! *I'm* here! *I'm* here!
The metallic rumble of the Green Line
can't drown her voice. She swings her hips,
clapping to the rhythm. I cross through a line of taxis
to avoid her. Now she is turning in grand circles,
her face lifted toward the tracks.
*Thank you, thank you, Lord of mine.*
I hum to myself, count sidewalk squares, anything
to escape the eye of her swirl. I quicken my stride
around the corner of Madison, until her voice is nothing
but a drift in the storm of buses and horns.
Yet at night, in the cool hour of unrest,
I feel her words rumbling through me
in a constant loop—*I thank you, Lord;*
*I thank you, Lord*—sparks flickering along my bones,
singeing the edges of my silent life.

# After the Annunciation

She couldn't sleep.
Lightning flickered in her head.
Her toes curled and uncurled.

Strange how the world
slumps on as usual, she thought.
Same brown mountains outside,
same cattle herd of snores
from her father.

But even she
couldn't think of angels now,
nor bellies nor saviors
nor blood. Just the images
from yesterday, when she walked
through the marketplace
and knew nothing.

The leprous old woman
crouched outside the city gate,
fingertips dissolving
like bread in the rain.

Two skeletal boys
poking through the mud
for shreds of fish.

Bruised and bejeweled
prostitutes hovering
by the leering vegetable vendors.

Everyone who is probably

lying awake like me, she thought.
Feeling too much. Wondering
why they have been chosen.
Waiting for the world
to start over.

# Mary at the Nativity

The angel said there would be no end
to his kingdom. So for three hundred days
I carried rivers and cedars and mountains.
Stars spilled in my belly when he turned.

Now I can't stop touching his hands,
the pink pebbles of his knuckles,
the soft wrinkle of flesh
between his forefinger and thumb.
I rub his fingernails as we drift
in and out of sleep. They are small
and smooth, like almond petals.
Forever, I will need nothing but these.

But all night, the visitors crowd
around us. I press his palms to my lips
in silence. They look down in anticipation,
as if they expect him
to spill coins from his hands
or raise a gold scepter
and turn swine into angels.

Isn't this wonder enough
that yesterday he was inside me,
and now he nuzzles next to my heart?
That he wraps his hand around
my finger and holds on?

# The Wedding at Cana

At first they stared in terror, the stream of water suddenly
flushing red, as if a fish had been speared in the cistern.

They steadied themselves on tables. They looked around,
awaiting the fire of angels to consume them. Eventually,

a guest cleared his throat and murmured, *Hey, we've got
a regular plague of wine here*, and they began to laugh, softly

at first, then wildly, lusciously, as the swallows ignited
their throats. The women rattled their tambourines;

the men stomped their feet on the dusty floor; the bridegroom
swung his wife to the ceiling. And Jesus whirled and whooped

in the middle of the room as his small, graying mother
poured the goblets like mad, wine spilling over her wrists.

# Mary at Calvary

### I. FRIDAY

Just below the nail head
on his left wrist—
the birthmark.

I see it through the blood.

We called it his storm cloud
when I bathed him as a child,
tracing the blurred edges.

I kissed it as he fell asleep,
watched it quiver
as he fastened boards,
saw it disappear
in the desperate grip of lepers.

The world waits
for my son's lungs to collapse.
I fix my eyes on the cloud.
It seems just a sunrise ago

I saw it for the first time,
a beautiful imperfection
resting on my breast
when our lives hung still and eternal
as this darkening sky.

### II. SATURDAY

All night I dream he is trudging
through sin, stepping over the carcasses

of stolen cattle, kicking piles of coins
withheld from laborers. He stumbles
over the bed linens of rape, the tattered clothes
of widows left to shiver on the streets.
He winces most at the bits of my fingernails
sticking in his feet, my midnight preoccupation
that he should have come down
when he had the chance
and be sitting here with me.

## III. SUNDAY

Nothing loves here. Guards stand still
as cypress trees in the thickening heat.
The disciples' footprints fill with sand.

God creates women for no reason
but grief. He can't cry himself
and needs a thousand vessels for his tears.

If I dug into this cracked earth,
I would find the piled bones of women
who lost husbands in battle
and children at birth,
who breathed out their last days
with darkness on their backs,
no commandments, visions or thrones.

Grief will be my legacy, too,
until I am forgotten. Like these lizards
scurrying over the tomb's stone.
The last star sinking into the light.

*The*
WOMAN
*at the*
WELL

# *Thirst*

Drifting in and out of fever, the child dreams of water.
Not the brown puddles twitching with mosquitoes

or the lukewarm drippings from the Red Cross pouches,
but the melted snow tracing diamond paths

down the mountains of his grandfather's stories.
He dreams of walking among the bongo

on the bamboo slope, spreading apart the reeds
and finding a stream. He crouches, cups his hands.

Water rolls through his lips, washes over
his gums, sinks into the grooves of his teeth.

He wakes crying for this stream to live in his body,
this water that once shimmered at the top of a peak

after falling through the sky, after shivering into snow,
after living in a cloud with a god somewhere.

# I Find the Messiah

on the carpet, in my daughter's sour blossoms of vomit
that I scrub with a shredded rag

inside the jammed printer, in the delicate cuts
collecting in the webs of my fingers

in the dried tendrils of millipedes that have squeezed
through the screens and dried up in the corners

on the blue clouds of mold sprouting over
the cucumbers in the refrigerator drawer

in the trilling crescendo of the Ford's loose fan belt
in the smoldering stars of grease in the oven

I find him—not on mountains or in fragrant temples—
but in the dusty village

where I search for a cup of crystalline water
and find his hair blowing wild in the wind.

# Before the Well

This man lying next to me is all
the men before. Hair and humid breath
traveling my body, perspiration dripping
on my breasts. He believes that I love
him. I wish I could awaken him
with whispers of wine and honey, fill the bed
with lilies and myrrh. I wish I could trace his lips
and feel something quiver in my blood.
Instead, I walk into the dark alone.
I close my eyes and imagine myself
beneath a canopy of apple trees, where nothing
touches me but the wind sweeping in
from the distant hills. Always clean and sweet.
Invisible and glimmering out of nowhere.

## After the Well

When she returned,
the men of the village
could no longer allow
their eyes to creep
into the hot, dark secrets
of her body.

She threw her shoulders back.
Her breasts and hips
took on the solid power
of granite carved
from the mountainsides.
And her hair was no longer
just a tangle of steamy pleasure,
but spread across her back
like a stand of cedar trees.

The men couldn't speak.
They watched her gather
the widows and prostitutes
and stretch her arm
toward Jacob's well.
The women followed her,
slowly lifting the veils
from their faces
as her faded blue dress
swept before them
like the holy sky.

# Sins of the Past

How effortlessly I tossed my ponytail over my shoulder and strutted over to Molly James, the slowest girl in sixth grade. She wore thick glasses and knee socks. Her sweater was embroidered with a hot pink M. She peered curiously at me. No one talked to Molly. But before she could even breathe *hello*, I said it: "You have to wear an M on your sweater because you're too stupid to know your own name." Her eyes widened. Kids laughed. She clamped her books to her chest.

"M is for Molly, M is for Molly," I sang, braces slinging saliva. "I bet there are M's on your socks"—and "M's on your pajamas"—and "M's on your underwear too." Tears quivered in her eyes. My stomach began to curl like one of those smoking, black snakes from the Fourth. But I had one more: "Maybe you should write M's all over your body so you always know who you are."

Only now do I imagine her climbing the steps to the bus, glancing down at her sweater as she sits alone, rides home, and goes upstairs without dinner. I see her staring at her bedpost with the sweater slung over it ("preppy," her mom said with hope in the fitting room) and waking to another day of trudging head-down to her classroom where we peek in the windows at the mystery teachers and their flock.

It's a wonder now that Molly is past thirty, perhaps looking into her own daughter's sullen face at the table. Of course, she would do anything to keep her from pain. I lie awake stunned by my own daughter's future, the grace and fear of watching her years unroll like a bolt of silk. How do I stop her from doing wrong? I try. I tell her everyone is lovely. I carry her around the yard to teach her about spring, the good birds building their nests in the treetops, the hyacinths pushing the dirt loose.

MARTHA

# The Bee Box

Years ago, I wanted to move like this:
furious, clumped in the brown flurry of work.

I would build the comb with thousands,
legs beaded with honey. How beautiful to fit,
to sink in that anonymous gold.

Now I am thirty. As a bee, I would be ten weeks,
scrambling toward death for the pulsing queen.

But I am told to appreciate life.
So I sit on my porch to stare at birds and grass,
while inside me legs scurry, abdomens bounce.

The hexagons wait to be filled.
I must fly out to one more patch of flowers.
I must seal the world shut with my wax.

# Martha and Mary

My sister clings to his feet
like a child, eyes brimming with wonder
as he tells of a place
where people soar like eagles
and flowers never die.

I drag the spoon through
the thickening stew, beat dirt
from the dining cushions,
fill the basin for his royal hands.

He tells me to relax and be like Mary
(who would let our guests suck sludge
from the bottom of wineskins).
Without me, there would be no bread
for the basket. We would fidget
and rub our aching heads,
too hungry to hear about our souls.
He would lift his cup to proclaim
the power of living water
and find it empty, forgetting who was there
to quietly fill it
hour after hour after hour.

# Lesson

1. Find the feet of God in a dark, quiet place.
   That pile of crumbling flower pots behind the garage should do.

2. Keep still. Do not clear the area of rocks or build an altar of flowers.
   Resist boisterous prayers or songs.

3. Wait. He will speak.

4. When you hear nothing, you will know He has spoken.

5. Watch the soil. Do not walk away.
   Vineyards tend to grow slowly.

6. Any time from one hour to one year you will see the seedlings emerge.
   Touch them. Listen to the cotyledons unfold.

7. Allow the vines to arch and wind around you.
   He will begin to drop grapes into your mouth.
   Accept these gifts.

8. Do not leave until he stands and sweeps the petals from his knees.

9. Go do the work you must do.

# July Afternoon

My daughter, just one, staggers
onto the lawn, finds a clover blossom
and holds her finger to the white sparks.
*Da-doe, da-doe,* she chants—her word
for flower—as the cabbage moths
take to full boil over the grass
and thin clouds cling to the rooftops.

I sit. She pushes the stem to the ground
and watches the flower spring back into place.
She pushes again, the flower springs.
She stomps her feet and squeals.

The rest of the world sags with doubt:
Oh, the sadness of such wasted time.
Every day the two of us
leave things the way we found them,
our voices heard by no one
but each other and the patient trees.

# Martha and Lazarus

Brother, what was it like to die?
Did your body drift into the black river of sleep?
Or did your heart suddenly drop to your chest like a stone?
Did you feel your muscles stiffen like ceiling beams,
then soften like roses in the rain?
Or did you feel nothing but your existence as a soul,
a circle of warmth suspended?
And what was it like to come back?
Did the air rush in like a wild gust,
or did you gasp through the burial linen?
Did the darkness pull apart like a curtain?
Did you roll over and cling to the earth like a child?
Could you even see, hear, stretch or cry?
Did God's weeping terrify?

JAIRUS' DAUGHTER

# Easter

At the sunrise service the pastor announces,
"Today you can decide to stop fearing death."
*No more fear*, I write on my program,
*4/11/06.* My husband peers over and nods.

In the car going home, I say nothing.
Of course, no one can *decide* such a thing.
But as I stare out the window, the trees
and brake lights and strip mall signs

melt into a garish swamp of the living.
Even my husband, humming as usual, is released
as I close my eyes and let death roll over me
like a carpet of sod—cool, green and breathing.

If I had to, I could die today. Never mind
the big rig with its tonnage of metal coils
swaying beside us, or the yellow sky in the distance
harboring funnel clouds. A clot could be nudging

its way to my heart; the gun in a dark lot waiting,
cocked. There would be a blip of pain,
then an opening rose of light—so bright,
I wouldn't see a thing.

# Jairus' Daughter

The girl is not dead,
but asleep.

See her blanket breathe?
See the new sweat
shiver on her brow?

Watch. Her lips have parted
to take in the blue air
of mourners' flutes.

Her eyes are flickering.
She is reaching
for his hand.

Because of her,
your hope will be stirred.

You will look for snowdrops
in the frost.

You will watch the roadside
body of a deer
and wait for an ear to flutter.

You will close the casket
and linger in the parlor,
listening for a knock.

# Jairus, After

He could do nothing but stare
as she twirled her hair around her fingers,

smelled the burial ointments and laughed,
blood blooming again in her cheeks.

And when she woke the next morning,
he told her, *No, don't fetch the water,*

so she just smiled and stretched
as he catalogued her fingernails and eyelashes,

the freckles on her neck, everything
he had almost lost. Then at dinner,

she began to whistle. Softly at first,
as she dipped her bread in the stew, then louder,

swaying in her chair. He raised
his eyebrows, but the whistling continued,

faster and higher, spinning in his ears
like a cloud of swallows in flight.

He squeezed his fists. A lentil dribbled
down her chin. Finally, she grinned,

threw her head back, and let the whistle whip
through the house like a windstorm.

*Slam*—he couldn't help it. He stared at his fists
as if he had dropped two heavy stones.

She stood up, shuddering, and crept back
to her bed in the corner. Jairus couldn't move.

He watched his daughter disappear inch by inch
as she drew the blanket over her body.

# Children of Near-Death

### EDWARD, DROWNING

Last day of fifth grade, I windmilled down to the waves.
    Water rolled toward me like giant green soda bottles.
    Seagulls screamed in the sky.

I dove. No more stuttering in class. No more stinky
    dodgeball courts, the cool kids lobbing
    at my face. I swam deeper,

a million pounds of water behind me. Kelp waved at me
    like a crowd in the grandstand.
    Wrapped around my arms and legs

till I couldn't get loose. Darkness. Then watching
    my body sway in the kelp. I was another body
    too, still swimming. The water got lighter,

like 7-Up. Fish whizzed by me as I raced toward the sun.
    I could see their blue skeletons and silver nerves
    and eggs with trembling fish inside.

Like seeing the future. Finally knowing something
    about the world. I was almost there,
    hand stretched. When someone

socked me hard in the stomach. Air rushed in
    like a gulp of mint ice cream.
    Water sprayed out of my mouth.

In front of the sun, a dozen kids looked down at me.
    I couldn't stop crying. I wanted the air. I wanted the water.
    I've wanted both ever since.

## CHRISTOPHER, ELECTROCUTION

I was a bad three-year-old,
Mom always yelling,

"Don't touch!" like when
I grabbed the vacuum cord

and chomped it
like a hungry rabbit.

Flash. A zipper unzipped
in my head. Blackness,

then all the shapes
I could never get right

falling like giant confetti:
blue triangles, red circles,

green squares flashing
and playing notes.

I could pick up the shapes
and say their names;

I could spin to the music,
throw my head back

and shout as loud as I could.
More colors fell

from the sky and melted
on my tongue like sugar.

This was a dream before

I knew about dreams.

This was sweeter than bedtime,
when mother tucked me in

with her rose-lotioned hands,
dropped kisses on my forehead

and sang my name until
I disappeared, another day

over and forgiven.

### KATIE, BIKE ACCIDENT

"Come," he says, and opens a creaky gate
to a field full of sunlight and flowers.
I'm not supposed to talk to strangers, especially men
who offer good things.  Mom's already
going to yell at me for riding past the corner of Oak Street.
So I run and run—that'll show the creep—away

from the miles of roses and poppies and daisies.
I run to my bike bent in half, wheels stuck together
like butterfly wings. I have to crawl back
into my body that lies beneath the crooked metal.
It's going to hurt, squeezing back into those sharp pieces of
        bone.
I don't want to pin my legs to the spokes again
or feel the slippery blood like finger paint on my face.
I want to twirl around in that field behind the gate.
*But you don't just do what feels good,* Mom says.
I know she's waiting for me, twisting the dishcloth.
Probably staring out the window. So I'll do the right thing.
I'll forget about the field. I'll crawl under the bike and gasp for
        air.

MARY MAGDALENE

# The Possession of Mary Magdalene

Pottery begged to be broken,
raked across her wrists.
Voices pulsed, *God is sorry,*
*God is sorry he made you.*
She scraped scabs
from her breasts—
*God is sorry—*
plucked eyelashes
and flicked them in the fire—
*God is sorry.*
And when she found her body
sufficiently fissured,
she drew her blanket over her like dusk
and sank into the steady hiss
of demons.

Follow the Nazarene
until he touches you,
a village woman told her.
Mary shook her head.
She had seen one of the touched.
The woman wrapped linen
around her wounds
until her body shone.
Strangers bellowed praises.
She wandered the roads
with a bewildered smile
well into the evening,
the fearful notes of her own singing
suspended in the dark.

# Mary Magdalene

In museums the world over
she scrambles to cover her nipples
with the fires of her hair,
gaping at the darkening skies
of Golgotha, cheeks flushed with sin.

Just a harlot, Pope Gregory declared
in 591, irritated that Peter slept in
that first Easter morning
and let a woman do his job.
Of *course* she repented by the tomb
day and night, having escaped a torrent of stones.

The listening priests nodded and smoothed
their mantles. They rose solemnly
and returned their fingers to the holy
water, kissed their crosses as her body
turned golden in their minds.

# Magdalene at the Crucifixion

I will knock out the nails

collect your blood
in these scattered leaves

funnel each drop
back into your wounds

I will catch your exhalations

that have escaped over
the mountains

trap them in my skirt
billow them back into your mouth

I can untie you then

you can bound down
stretching and smiling

go back to when
your body was a mystery

feet skimming the rivers
veins swimming with stars

# The Empty Tomb

*—John 20*

That *woman* was the first word spoken
must have taken even the angels by surprise,

who were used to bringing their fiery glory
down to the clanging swords of battlefields,

to priests tugging at their beards
in lamentation, to voices thundering in temples

and muscles hefting stones from mountaintops,
not to a trembling woman whose hair clung

to her neck with tears, who for a moment
held the souls of the nations like a basket of figs.